Persuasion

The Secret to be Persuasive and to Have Influence at the Workplace

Bruce Walker

Contents

Introduction

Influence.

Have you ever met that person who seems to be a natural "leader?" He or she will make a suggestion and all others think it's a great idea. Of course, the fact that you made the same suggestion ten minutes earlier and no one listened made this situation all the more pointed.

Most people can't fully articulate what makes one person more influential than another. Is it charisma? Offhand, you might case a better and more expensive education. Neither of these seems to be. Yet, when pressed, they'll shrug their shoulders and say, "I'll know it when I see it."

And indeed, they do. You probably do, too. All you have to do is look around you. There always seems to be one person who others turn to for advice from any task as large at launching a project to something as small as the wording of a business letter. These people carry influence around with them like most people carry their wallets.

Then there are other individuals in the same workplace who may possess twice the knowledge and are more qualified to answer the questions but no one asks them.

Normally, you would expect the team or department leader to be the most influential person in the group. But that's not always the case. There are those cases in which the most influential person does not carry the title leader, was never appointed as leader and ironically doesn't even care to have that title.

Influence is Leadership

Simply because a person has been given the title of leader – from that of a small group on the plant floor to the upper echelons of the corporate structure – doesn't necessarily mean he or she carries any natural influence with anyone.

John Maxwell, who spent a good portion of his career studying leaders and leadership, offers a simple explanation for what many see as a conundrum. "Leadership is influence," he said, "and influence is leadership, nothing more, nothing less."

Too many individuals have been appointed leaders but realize when they "get in charge" that the dynamics of the group have not changed. If they weren't seen as influential before they are given that raise or put in charge of a project, these same individuals aren't going to sudden be given superhero influential powers.

About all the title of leader provides them, usually is some form of superficial prestige and or artificial power. But the title, itself, fails to install one crucial item upon this individual: influence.

A leader who finds he has no followers, according to Maxwell, is "a person going for a long walk." Similarly, another person has described the typical leader as a person who sees which way the crowd is headed and then runs to catch up to it so he can eventually walk in front of it.

Leaders should be, by their very nature, influential. People naturally want to follow true leaders, whether they carry the title or not. They'll even abandon a corporate-appointed leader if individuals don't perceive him as a natural spearhead of the group or team. People are willing and eager to following a person who is influential if they believe that individual can take them where they need to go.

Think for a moment about some of the so-called leaders in your life. Are they real leaders? Think about your supervisor at work or group project leader? They very well may carry the title of leader and even bask in it. But if the people this person is intended to lead don't perceive him as such, then he'll have a hard time gaining influence over them to make his point.

Perhaps this so-called leader lacks in the delicate ways of interacting with people. It could be that he or she lacks the charisma, the backbone or the character. Sometimes leaders are great people as far as human beings don't have the traits that make a great leader. Sometimes it's simply just these so-called authority figures aren't working toward the same causes as the "followers" or aren't delivering the results they promised.

The Importance of Being Influential at the Workplace?

Most of us, either secretly or openly, would like to be influential in the workplace. Some individuals reading this book now may already have the title of "leader" but may be lacking "followers." If you find that you've recently been promoted to a leadership position but can't decipher the code of getting your employees to believe in you and ultimately take your lead, then this book was written with you in mind.

If you don't have the title of leader yet, but would eventually be thrilled to receive it, this volume is also written for you. In either case, you need to learn how to be influential. Usually, it's better to learn this before someone sticks that title on your sleeve after you've learned the fine art of influencing others. But, keep in mind it's never too late to learn this. In other words, there's still time to learn exactly what makes a great leader and, more importantly, adopt these traits and mannerisms to your personality even if you've had the title for years.

If you already are a leader, but find your efforts fruitless or ineffectual, then you, too, can take the concepts in this book and adapt what you need to increase your sphere of influence. Once people at work begin to notice the change in you, then you'll see how your standing rises not only with those who you're supervising but with your supervisors as well.

What will they discover you've evolved into a true leader? What will you learn in this book about being a true leader? You'll learn – maybe for the first time in your life – that you have the ability to effect positive change. You'll discover a new level of enthusiasm for your work. In the process, this enthusiasm will be contagious and every one of your followers will feel the same way, naturally. Others will discover your trustworthiness. In a nutshell, you will be that person who others believe in and come to for advice.

If you're already a hard worker on your team, that will carry you far. But, if at the same time you can make yourself valuable to others, they'll be indebted to you. If your colleagues believe you actually care about them then, they, in turn, will undoubtedly be loyal to you.

There is no better time to make the decision to be influential. The world needs strong leadership – and not only in the corporate world. Look around you. True leaders seem to be lacking everywhere. At the city level – not only politics but in civic matters as well. If, after reading this book you will not only be a more influential person, but you'll be a leader. Don't be surprised if many begin to recognize you as the natural leader you are.

The Four Fundamental Principles of Influence

Let's get one thing straight from the start, the ability to influence people has nothing to do bribing people to do what you want them to do, cajoling them into believing a certain way or even threatening them. Instead, it has everything to do with sincerely caring about others and searching for a way that everyone feels as if they've been a part of a productive team experience.

In this book, you'll learn the four fundamental principles of learning the art of influencing others. Not only that, but you'll see how these principles -- social proof, commitment and consistency, liking, and authority – are the most valuable traits and habits you can develop for your new role of being an influence on your colleagues.

Now, more than ever before, corporations are searching for leaders. But more than that, companies of all levels are looking for those individuals who are influential with their colleagues – with, at the very least, leadership potential.

Your ability to help influence others within your company to make crucial decisions, to persuade others to accept the latest concepts, see the advantages of taking a certain amount of risk, of even helping others to think out of the box could make the difference between staying in the same job classification indefinitely or climbing up your company's ladder. It could make the difference between ultimately having an occupation and enjoying a successful long-term career.

Are you ready to get started? In Chapter One, we'll talk about the necessity of being influential regardless of your career or your interests.

Chapter 1: Why It's Important to be an Influential Person at the Workplace

When was the last time you scrutinized your workplace? No, I'm not talking about the furniture or the electronic equipment. Take a good, long look at your supervisor or the person officially tagged as the "leader" of your team or department. Now, carefully examine the attitudes and actions of your colleagues.

Who do you consider the natural leaders in your workplace? Is it the officially sanctioned supervisor with a good title, a corner office, whose words are the voice of authority?

Be honest now. Is there anyone among your colleagues whose voice naturally carries influence? It seems like every department has at least one person – usually not the supervisor – who appears to wield the influence.

Years ago, there was a television commercial for a brokerage firm, E.F. Hutton. Perhaps some of you remember it. Their motto was "When E.F. Hutton speaks, people listen." That is the essence of a true leader. Who among your colleagues, if anyone, carries this type of weight?

Sometimes this is the individual who has the ear of the supervisor. Sometimes it isn't. But you can tell, he'll make a great supervisor someday if given the opportunity.

Your colleague is what's known as an unspoken influential leader. Many individuals point to this person – not the supervisor – when they say, "I want to be able to lead like he does. I want to be influential. Eventually, I want to be the supervisor. A good, effective supervisor."

Even with all the technology you may master in the process of learning your job, being proficient in computer skills and other electronics doesn't necessarily guarantee promotions within your career.

What it takes to be a True Leader

A person who can not only guide others in doing their job but actually encourage and inspire others is a true leader. This is a person with influence. Ironically, many times, it isn't the officially sanctioned leader.

"That's what I want," you say to yourself. Then you pause for a moment. It's just a matter of learning how to "get" people to listen to me. How in the world does that happen?"

Indeed, how do you become an influential leader? Many individuals believe there's a type of "magic" or mysticism involved. Imagine for a moment, if you were that person. Your words, regardless of how carelessly you toss them out of your mouth, are considered important.

If you were an influential leader the instant you said anything, it would be branded as legitimate and would be considered the truth. You can hear the conversations around the water cooler now. "But that's not what (insert your name here) said. He said . . . "

If you make a prediction, they'll be people waiting for it to come true. There would probably be an equal number of people who expect the prediction to blow up in your face.

The bottom line is that when you do reach that level of influence (and you know you will with the help of this book) you'll have to remind yourself every day of the responsibility that goes along with that power.

Ask any person of influence and they'll all tell you down to a person that building influence is hard work. But in the next breath, they'll add that the rewards are well worth it.

It's only right that before we cover the four major principles of acquiring influence that we spend a few moments on how it may affect your standing in the first place.

Influence isn't some cloak that's bestowed on you like a graduate gown after you finish a course. I've worked at several corporations that would give the persons who they appointed supervisors courses in leadership. It always seemed backward to me. If I were in charge, I would seek out natural leaders, then have them learn more with those classes and confidently send them off to learn their jobs.

Every leader knows that becoming a leader is a bit like building a house. You build it brick by brick. Leaders are developed by cultivating influence person by person. You can't influence anyone by sitting at your desk all day ignoring them then expect them to pay attention to your words at the next meeting.

It's possible that may happen, but it's highly unlikely. No, you've got to develop a personal relationship with your colleagues.

I worked in a subsidiary of General Motors at one time. The plant manager came down on the floor every day, walked through each department, and walked up to every person who had a person that day. He'd ask about family and any birthday plans.

He was a true leader. He knew how to build influence. I often wondered how he did it until I became a supervisor of one of the lines myself. He'd stop to ask me who so-and-so was and made sure he knew something of his background. Then he would walk straight up to that person as if the manager had known all along who he was.

Before you even start about how he "cheated," you need to know that plant manager cultivated more good feelings doing that. We as a group would have walked through hell with him had he asked us to.

Of course, that's not the only reason he was a good leader, but it's a great illustration of how leadership is won one individual at a time. It's a lesson I'll never forget.

In fact, to be a true leader, you have to spend at least as much time "on the floor" listening to your employees as you do lock away in your office. Your goal is not only to listen, to take in what these people are telling you. Build relationships with them

The process of being a true leader and wielding honest influence is personal. Very personal.

Every Step Must Include Trust and Respect

Are you beginning to understand that every step of your constructing your influence is based on trust and respect? There's no way around it. There are no shortcuts.

At the same time, you're building your "house of influence," others will be judging your actions. People – especially those who work with you – are smart. They can tell if you're being sincere or if you're going through the motions just to get a promotion. If everything you're doing is a façade, you'll get caught. Guaranteed. So you might as well as start off and end up sincere.

What are people judging you on? They're carefully eyeing you up on how well your actions line up with your words. If you "promise" a colleague or an employee something, and don't follow through because you forgot or it was an impossible promise, then don't expect them to think of you as a leader. Or influential for that matter.

As a matter of fact, some sociologists suggest that promises not kept may be the biggest reason why people fail to gain influence. Be careful what you promise others. It's much better to underestimate your ability to acquire something for others and actually get it than overestimating and failing.

This process of gaining trust of your colleagues is an arduous task. But it's also one that's well worth the work. As they begin to trust you and realize you're a person of your word, that when your influence begins to grow. You'll eventually see that the initiatives you're taking are actually beginning to take hold.

You're not only being scrutinized by your employees, but by your supervisors as well. Soon, they too will sit up and take notice that problems in your department or team are handled without panic and nearly effortlessly.

The reason? You've already created the relationships required for action to be taken in a timely manner. Your colleagues know that if they help solve this "crisis" that you'll remember and help them when they need it.

It really is that simple.

First, though, you need to know the four principles of gaining influence and how they work. The first is social proof and we discuss it in the following chapter.

Chapter 2: Most of Us are Followers

The principle of social proof, or as it's sometimes referred to informational social proof, is fairly simple. If a person doesn't know the correct way to respond in a social situation, he'll naturally follow the lead of those he sees around him. He takes his cues and guidance from whomever he is with at the time.

It's simple enough, but yet, you can see right away it just might be a bit dangerous. When you do this you're making an implicit assumption. You're assuming that those individuals know how to respond. Dangerous, yes. But at the same time comforting. At least you won't be alone if you've responded wrong.

You may never have needed to use it. Then again there are situations when it can involve a matter of life or death. Social proof is often used in times of crisis or uncertainty. In an emergency or disaster, you usually don't have the time to think through the correct response.

All of us, at one time or another, has experienced this. When we are faced with an unfamiliar situation, we look around and defer to others for implicit guidance.

Another way social proof is put into use is when people see those with similar interests or those close to their age, their sex or some other traits they can relate to doing something.

Perhaps you've even done it yourself. When you've been at a loss of exactly how to react in a social or work situation, it's only natural to look around and gravitate to a person you can relate to. This is a fairly common phenomenon and might be something you've already noticed.

Research, in fact, has substantiated this casual observation. When this action occurs at the high school level, it's very often pejoratively labeled as peer pressure. Surprisingly, peer pressure doesn't end with graduation. The people who we're closest to or we've identified as important to us and meaningful in our lives in some form are the first ones we turn to in order to help us make decisions.

Have you ever heard the statistic that each of us is a composite of five of our closest friends? It may be these five individuals you'll turn in order how to react in unfamiliar circumstances.

Research has also a revealed that you're more likely to ask or mimic a person who has expertise in the area in question when you're at a loss of how to act. The fact that they know more than you set them up in your eyes as the "expert." Therefore, they should be able to guide you in the proper response.

No Leader Nearby, Then What?

But let's say there is no expert close by, no one you know and not a single person you can really identify with using any type of standard demographics. Then what do you do? Psychologists tell us that most people will gladly follow what the majority of the other people are doing.

The more people who find an idea or action acceptable, the more the uncertain observer looking for guidance will adopt the point of view of the majority of those around him whether he can find a similarity with them or not.

Perhaps, this is the most important of all the discoveries, for it explains the influence of the mass media – television, radio, internet among other forms of communications. The greater the number of people you watch reacting in a certain set of circumstances on the internet, for example, the more likely that reaction is adopted by those who would otherwise be at a loss of how to respond.

If you're not convinced of these "casual observations" let's examine just a few of the psychological studies performed in testing the theory of social proof. Let's start with one of the most significant and famous of the students. It involves something as mundane as "canned laughter."

If you're not familiar with this term, it's the total unrealistic laugh track that's used in television situation comedies to tell you, the home viewer, when you've just heard a joke. It's inserted in the soundtrack to trigger your own laughter.

Regardless of what you may think of it, this laugh track really does induce individuals to laugh. Not only that, but the results of experiments reveal that people laugh longer and more often when they hear the fake laughter.

But the influence doesn't end then. Participants in studies were asked to rate the material for its humor. Those portions of the program in which the tract was used were rated as funnier than those without the canned laughter. This suggests the researchers said that it even makes the poor jokes which would normally fall flat, seem funny.

Why? It would seem that if you don't find something funny, some obviously fake laughter prompt you not only to laugh but to rate the material funnier than what it really is?

You probably already know the answer. According to the theory of social proof, we determine what is correct – and evidently what is funny – by gauging the reaction of others. The fact that even fake laughter stimulates an automatic response in people points to the possibility that what we hear (scientists would call this auditory cues) are potent because our responses come from a subconscious level.

Even the theory that individuals take many of their social cues from those they view as most of them has been verified through research. In fact, according to research, this is when it "operates most powerfully," when we see people we can identify with.

Marketers have already learned from this. Watch ads for diet programs and you'll see ordinary people – just like you – who have lost weight on one diet program or supplement or another. Direct marketing copywriters love to include these "testimonials" into their ads because they're effective. In some instances, they're the "tipping point" for many readers who otherwise would look with cynicism on the advertisement.

It may also account for, some researchers posit, the popularity of reality television. Those involved in these shows were not actors before they appeared on them. They were – and are – average individuals just like you.

Social proof is just one of the four principles you can learn to help you gain the influence and power of persuasion that's critical to your success in the twenty-first-century workplace.

Once you know how you can use the next principle, commitment and consistency to help you gain favorable influence and increase your power of persuasion, you'll see how these four puzzle pieces eventually fit snugly together. That's the topic of the next chapter, commitment, and consistency.

Chapter 3: Commitment and Consistency

"I said what I meant and I meant what I said."

It's more than a little unorthodox to quote a Dr. Seuss book when writing on influence. But in his book, "Horton Hatches an Egg," a loyal elephant named Horton agrees to sit on Mayzie's egg while she flies to parts unknown.

The plot isn't important, but the quote is. This is probably the easiest and quickest way to introduce the principle of "commitment and consistency." Regardless of your cynicism, the vast majority of people want their words to match with their actions.

Most individuals don't like to have to back out of deals. Once they have committed to a certain intention – especially in writing or verbally – they are less likely to change their minds. In a nutshell, the majority of people try to be consistent in their commitments.

The key element behind the theory of this principle is the power of commitment. Once people promise to do something, they then begin to act in ways that reinforce that commitment. As soon as they "take a stand," they, much like Horton in the Dr. Seuss children's book, will do everything within their power to see it through. That means they purposely practice behavior that is "stubbornly consistent" with their commitment.

An interesting example of the "commitment and consistency" principle at work is revealed through the results of a study conducted by social scientist Anthony Greenwald in 1987. The results are still remarkable thirty years later. The day before an election he asked people whether they had planned to vote. Not only that, but he asked them to explain why they answered the way they did. He also had a control group to whom he didn't pose that question.

Everyone he talked to said they were going to vote. The following day, nearly 87 percent of those who "publicly committed" to voting actually did. Of the group that wasn't asked only 60 percent actually voted.

Getting customers or co-workers to publicly commit to something makes them more likely to follow through with an action or a purchase. Ask your team members if they'll support your next initiative and have them explain why.
There's another key to this principle. When people make a commitment in front of others, they're even more likely to work hard to keep from breaking it. Perhaps when you think of public commitments your mind first turns to the most serious of them, declarations of commitment in the marriage vows, a baptism, or a bar mitzvah.

How you Phrase your Question Matters

Believe it or not, the way you phrase your request for a commitment also has a potent effect on whether individuals feel committed. Instead of just asking an individual to "call me if you have to cancel our dinner," the odds are more likely he actually will if you phrase the request so he has to answer it with the word yes. In this case, you'd ask, "Would you please call if you need to cancel?"

Interestingly enough, this particular principle has a second part. If you can influence individuals to commit to something small, then it's easier for them to transform that into a large commitment.

Results of research provide ample evidence of this with something as simple as wearing a cancer awareness pin. That's a small, seemingly innocuous action. Once a group of individuals agreed to this and wore the pin for a while, they were then asked to donate monetarily to the cause. Those who had worn the pin for any length of time were more likely to make a donation.

So what's really at work here? Why do individuals feel the need, after talking with a complete stranger, to follow through on a commitment they made? There's a secondary principle at work and it's called alignment. As human beings we actually need our beliefs, values and actions to all work together – to be aligned. Psychologists call what we feel when all of these aren't aligned cognitive dissonance. We know something's not right and both our minds and sometimes even our bodies tell us so -- quite loudly.

If we fail to align our actions with our beliefs sometimes a strange thing occurs. We find ourselves actually changing our belief system in order to accommodate the commitment we made.

These ideas are predicated on the fact that the person must feel as if he freely chose his commitment. He can't feel as if he had been coerced into doing this simply out of a sense obligation. Then this fails to be a free choice and looks more like manipulation on the part of those trying to get the commitment.

We've all probably felt manipulated at one time or another. At the very least when you were being urged to purchase something, let's say a car, you weren't quite ready to commit to. The salesman, if he's too aggressive, can appear to be manipulating you into buying it just so he can get the commission. If you feel as if the salesperson is forcing you into an agreement, then you are less tied to it and are much more apt to back out of the deal.

What Does This Mean for the Workplace?

While one-on-one meetings with your colleagues or your employees are great, when it comes to getting people to commit to something, the effect will be greater if you ask for their support in a meeting. Don't ask for a huge vow initially, though. Remember if you can get your colleagues to agree to something small, the larger agreements will naturally occur later.

But more than that, go around the room and specifically ask each individual if he or she could support the project. Be sure to phrase the question so they have to answer with either a yes or a no.

When they answer yes, ask them why. They have not only promised their support verbally, but they've done it in public.

The other aspect of this principle you need to remember is that influence isn't and should never be confused with manipulation. The latter implies getting your way through changing the behavior of others – often at their expense. More often than not manipulation involves exploiting your colleagues. In some instance, it can even involve abuse and deception.

That is not what leaders do. And if you manipulate others, then you probably can give up on your goals of becoming a true leader – for one thing, you may never be able to regain the trust of those you with whom you work.

In the next chapter, you'll learn more about the principle simply called "liking."

Chapter 4: The Power of The Halo Effect

Seems incredulous that a principle that sounds more like what people are asked to do on Facebook and other social media could actually be a serious psychological principle at your disposal in order to gain social influence.

According to this rule, individuals prefer to agree with those they not only already know, but truly like. If someone sincerely likes you as a person, your chances of influencing them increase.

But that's not all. It appears that people would rather be most likely to like to those people who are physically attractive and most like themselves.

If neither of those two options is available, then most people prefer to work with those who offer them compliments.

The "Halo Effect"

Some psychologists refer to this as the "halo effect." Many individuals see an attractive person and naturally assume that he or she is talented, kind, honest and intelligent.

The results of research performed in Canada several years ago confirms this. It occurred during their national elections. Those candidates who were perceived as being more attractive than their opponents received two and half times the number of votes. This occurred despite the fact that when questioned, voters said that physical good looks didn't influence their choices.

Sadly, this tendency to endow attractive people with a host of good qualities, whether you know them or not extends into the court of law. Physically good looking individuals are more likely to get favorable verdicts than the less attractive individuals. Even sadder, psychologists see this principle of "liking" developing when children are in elementary school.

We like those who are like us

Remember the adage "birds of a feather flock together?" According to the concepts of influence, it may be truer than you ever imagined. Scientific studies, while they didn't purposely set out to prove the birds-of-a-feather theory, did discover that we are drawn to those persons who are most similar to us. Does this sound familiar?

In researching the theory of "social proof" which we talked about in an earlier chapter, we're more likely, when faced with the unfamiliar terrain, to look around and follow the lead of those people who we believe are most similar to us.

But let's take this one step further, people even tend to like those who dress most like them. This principle helps to explain the myriad of uniforms as well as unofficial dress codes in school.

Complimenting others

We've all done it. We've complimented someone on their new hair style, a new article of clothing or just about anything else. When we're at work we sometimes tell them how they've done a great job handling this account or conducting themselves in a departmental meeting.

According to the principle of "liking," the power that flattery carries is immense. A study conducted in North Carolina, for example, evaluated the effects on men when met with positive, negative or mixed comments. The comments were made by a series of various individuals.

It worked like this. The evaluator who only doled out praise was like most by the men. No surprise there. What was eye-opening, though, was the fact the men liked him even though they knew he had a hidden agenda, as it were, for giving a compliment. Not only that, but the comment didn't even need to be accurate to be influential. When the flatterer praised others for items that weren't true, the individuals liked him every bit as much.

It seems that contrary to the cute little remark, "flattery will get you nowhere," it really can take people places.

The lesson for you, the person attempting to gain influence, is not to go out and carelessly give compliments. The lesson is that if you give a compliment be sure you're sincere. Stay true to your values. Doling out compliments in exchange for influence is perilously close to crossing the line from being a leader to being a manipulator.

In the following chapter, we'll see how, as a society, we're taught to defer to authority and what that means for your leadership potential.

Chapter 5: Perceived as an Important Person

.

Within two hours, a television reporter had collected $10,000 in cash and checks from complete strangers. How did he do it? The entire episode is a grand lesson in the unspoken, implicit power of authority, one of the principles in gaining influence.

This following example is the best definition of how the principle of authority works. It's a shocking revelation of how trusting people can be when faced with someone who they believe is in a position of authority.

He was easily identified as a guard. He wore a uniform, a badge and even carried a baton. He placed the sign on the ATM machine outside the bank. It read, "Out of Order – Give Deposits to Guard on Duty." The sign also had a large, gold badge printed on it.

One by one, customers would approach and read the sign. The guard smiled and asked them if they had planned to make a deposit. When they said yes, he offered to take the money for them.

Person after person handed the guard cash and conducted private transactions with this man they didn't know. They not only gave this man, who turned out as you've probably guessed already, a television reporter checks, revealed PIN numbers and other private information usually shared by no one.

The depositors upon hearing the news were amazed. The reporter asked them why they even considered doing it. Down to a person, they answered that the person had a uniform and a badge. Basically, he looked like an authority figure.

The Technical Definition of the Principle

While this narrative is a marvelous illustration of the authority principle, the principle itself does have a definition. It states that people are deferential – to a fault as we've just seen -- to those who appear to be in a position of power.

The power of authority isn't bestowed solely on those who wear uniforms. It could be anyone who proclaims he has more power or even knowledge than you. It's those folks with impressive credentials or it could even be those who just carry an air of confidence about them.

The bottom line is this: when an individual appears to be in a position of authority, then we usually act as if they were, regardless of what their actual position may be.

Usually, there are symbols or signs individuals "carry with them" which clue us into their heightened status. Below are three of the most common:

Titles

Those individuals who put the word doctor in front of their names or Professor in front of it. Those who have the initial Ph.D. following their names. And then there are those who are routinely referred to as president or chairman.

Clothing

You can identify a doctor nearly instantly in a hospital because he or she wears a white coat. Many priests and ministers dress in black. Some even wear clerical collars. Police officers routinely wear blue and those who command respect in the business world usually dress in gray suits.

Trappings

For the lack of any better word, trappings are those auxiliary items that go with a uniform or a form of dress. Doctors will often have stethoscopes around their necks. Ministers may carry Bibles or wear prayer beads, and police officers carry guns.

Why Do We Defer to Authority?

Throughout our entire childhood and into adulthood, we've been taught to respect people in charge. Think about it. As children, we were surrounded by our parents and teachers and other adults who were bigger, more knowledgeable about life and vastly more experienced than we were. In college, we learned in classrooms taught by individuals who had doctorate degrees. Normally, we sat silently and furiously took notes as they gave lectures – spewed out ideas and concepts we were supposed to learn. As we grew into adulthood, we naturally deferred authority to police officers, medical doctors.

In essence, we were taught to do what we were told. If we didn't? Well, I'm sure your parents had their own brand of punishment to mete out. If you didn't do what your teachers said at school, you were sent to the principal's office. An even more intimidating authority figure.

You can see how it escalates from there. Once we're adults, we defer to our medical doctors. Or when we're searching for information on nutrition or diet, we turn to others with the proper credentials. In fact, if you watch the commercials carefully more often than not everything we've talked about that allows you to spot an authority figure immediately is there.

A person with a title. The right clothing to convey authority and all the trappings, including the equipment.

If you're feeling right about now you're being deceived or manipulated, don't. This instant deferring to authority is not only common, but it's natural. And in many ways in this society, it's also beneficial. Imagine trying to wend your way through life without any guidance or insight from authorities.

In fact, our culture has respect for authority that is both immediate and powerful. This means that those who wield even a small amount of authority can use this principle to get cooperation more often than what you think.

But to have authority figures who guide us and make recommendations to us is actually a good thing. If we needed to verify every word of every sentence of some the commercials on television or direct mail material that comes to your house, it would be very time-consuming.

Not only that, but if there weren't people with those proper credentials, how would you even begin to evaluate some of these things. Psychologists like to call decisions in this fashion as a "decision heuristic," or a social "shortcut to make a decision."

Let's face it, life can get complicated. It's difficult to personally evaluate all elements of all situations. Sooner or later, we learn that by relying on specialists and those in authority, we may be doing ourselves a real favor when we turn to others, more knowledgeable than ourselves for certain types of information.

If not Authority, Then Credibility

Yes, if you can establish authority in your circle, that's great. But did know you can take a giant step forward from this and become credible to others. Establishing credibility is actually quite simple. Much psychological research has been performed in this area and four basic elements need to be present in order for you to present yourself as a credible spokesperson either at home or at work. They are expertise, trustworthiness, similarity, and physical attractiveness.

While you can probably guess the first two are the most important, all four of them work together and feed off each other. Let's examine each part of the concept of credibility in its own right briefly.

Expertise

Expertise is simply possessing the knowledge that is needed at the moment. Scrutinize your background. Evaluate any specialized education you may have in the area in question. Have you any experience in the topic they're talking about? Perhaps you already displayed a level of competency in this area already. Think about the successful experiences you've already had in this area.

Trustworthiness

Do others feel as if they can trust you? Do you know if others within your workplace trust you? Before you answer yes to that, keep one thing in mind. They will find you trustworthy depending on what they believe think your intentions are. In effect, people want to know why you choose to believe the way you do.

If they feel you have a hidden agenda or an ulterior motive for helping them, you may find yourself losing credibility and in effect some authority. In fact, scientists have two terms that show up time and again. If your colleagues believe. In fact, scientists have two terms that show up time and again.

If your colleagues believe you suffer from a "knowledge bias" than they believe you've experience events in your life that prevent you from looking at the project from an objective viewpoint.

If you're told you have a "reporting bias," your co-workers are saying that only telling them what they want to hear – not the entire story. Before you go much further in advancing your case at work, you should pause and acknowledge that there are always two sides to every argument.

In order to become trustworthy in the eyes of your colleagues then they must know that you're presenting both sides of every case and that you must be doing so in an impartial manner.

Similarity

There's that word again. It occurs in just about everything of any importance when it comes to establishing influence, and the principle of being seen as an authority figure is no exception.

Why? It's really simpler than you might believe. We listen to and weigh information we receive from someone we like more heavily than from someone we don't care for. It's so much easier to ignore information coming from people we really don't respect than from an individual who we believe is thinking proper – and quite a bit like us as it turns out.

We may not do it on a conscious level, but we tend to ask questions of relationship to the person who's attempting to gain the influence. We wonder if he thinks like us, looks like us and all the other criteria we've used to designate similarity, is there some validity then to what he's saying.

The more we can answer yes to these questions, then the more credibility he gains in our eyes. And, of course, the more likely we are to accept his ideas.

Physical Attractiveness

Finally, the fourth component of establishing credibility is that of physical attractiveness. This isn't an easy one for some of us to accept. Nonetheless, it's been proven that good looking individuals are considered smarter than less attractive people. We are more likely to pay attention of someone who is good looking than to someone who isn't.

Logically we tell ourselves we're above such shallow thinking. Our emotional minds and subconscious minds, though, keep us tied to such thinking.

For starters, if a person is good looking, then we tend to view him as something called the "halo effect." This is that pleasant feeling that settles down into us whenever we're with him. But more than that, study after study show that attractive individuals are perceived as being overall better communicators.

There's only one exception to this last component. There's such a thing as being "too attractive." That occurs when the individual's physical looks actually distract from his or her ability to establish influence.

Now that you've familiarized yourself with the four major principles of gaining influence, it's time to start applying them in the workplace. The following chapter includes seven of the most important methods guaranteed to work in any workplace or business.

Chapter 6: Persuasion and Manipulation at The Workplace

The power to persuade is like a house of cards.

Indeed, it's a very real power and with it comes to a great responsibility.

Don't kid yourself. The power to persuade is, indeed, a power that should never be taken or used lightly. It may take individuals years to cultivate this asset, but it only takes one faux pas on your part to lose everything.

You've just learned the four principles that go into gaining influence – especially in the workplace. These principles are critical to you achieving your personal and professional goals. No one needs to tell you that the more influence you can wield in your workplace the more successful you'll become.

You'll be the go-to person for many people who are trying to solve problems, deal with mistakes and even manage personal conflicts on the work floor or in the office. And if you're a supervisor and you've gained influence with your employees, then you can expect to be respected and appreciated.

If you're an influential personal in the upper echelons of your company your opinions – either rightly or wrongly – carry more weight than others.

When you're using it, though, you must be careful. It's a trait that can take years to cultivate, but can be lost nearly instantly with one careless word or action.

Applying the Principles

Once you know what's involved in influence, how do you apply these four principles in the workplace to make you a valuable leader?

Below are seven simple steps you can take to help kick start your influence at work. If you're not already applying these steps now, then slowly introduce them into your office routine. As you do so, you'll be surprised at how easy it'll be to gain the influence you desire.

1. Develop a trusting relationship with your colleagues

Trust is the ultimate conduit through which influence flows. If people don't trust you, they sure won't pay much attention to your ideas or actions. Trust comes in many forms. Perhaps you tend to exaggerate facts at meetings. After the meeting, someone fact checks what you've said only to discover that many of your figures are off. Perhaps the figures are correct, but you've mispresented them.

If your colleagues trusted you going into the meeting, once they discover this, they may no longer listen to your opinions at the next meeting.

Trust is also built by meeting promises. If you don't think you can keep a promise to an employee – regardless of how small and insignificant it may appear to you, tell him up front. If you intend to try to help him, let him know. But don't promise a thing unless you know it's a "sure thing."

2. Become a reliable person

If you're not already viewed as reliable by those around you, it's time to start improving that image. Becoming a reliable person is not that difficult, but it does take some time, especially if that's one area up to now you haven't been very good at.

You need to be consistent in what you do. That includes finishing your tasks on time, every day. Once individuals see they can trust (there's that word again) that your actions line up with your intentions, then you slowly become the person your colleagues will rely on.

3. Assert yourself

As a person of leadership, it's only natural to assume that you'll need to be assertive. What you want to avoid at all costs, though, is being aggressive.

When you're assertive you'll notice that your colleagues and supervisors will take notice of your concepts and plans. This is especially true when, as in the typical workplace, you're vying for visibility – especially in meetings. It's all too easy for your voice to get drowned out.

Don't make the mistake, though, of confusing being aggressive with being assertive. An example of being assertive is presenting your ideas to people with confidence. But, you don't want to appear overconfident because that could be misconstrued for arrogance. Presenting your ideas with any more "confidence" beyond that could additionally be mistaken for aggressiveness.

Considering the fine long among these three – assertiveness, arrogance, and aggressiveness – you should always measure your words before speaking. If you're speaking to others within the company who you don't know very well, then you need to be doubly careful. It doesn't take but a slip of the tongue or somebody movement for others to misjudge your intentions.

4. Exert flexibility

This step to gaining influence may seem to contradict the one before it. Practicing both of them may not be the easiest thing, but it's possible. Flexibility is light years beyond "waffling." Waffling is when you apparently change your beliefs depending on whom you're speaking with.

Flexibility, on the other hand, is when you acknowledge the position of another and try to reach some form of compromise without either of you surrendering your values. If you appear too rigid and refuse to even hear what your colleagues or employees have to say about the matter, you may eventually gain a reputation as a "tyrant." That's certainly the farthest thing from a leader.

5. Be a personal, approachable individual

It only makes sense. Influence, as we've seen, is built on developing professional relationships with people one person at a time. It's about finding out what's important to them and then keeping that in mind. Someday you may be able to use your influence to help them attain what they want.

But as a serious leader, you can't really be "friends" with your employees. You need to keep some distance. Being a leader with influence means walking many fine lines, as we've already seen. This is just one more of them

It seems counter-intuitive to try to cultivate influence by distancing yourself from others. If people don't know you, then how can they come to trust you? At meetings, if you're not known you stand in danger of becoming just another "talking head" as they say. Yes, your ideas may be good, but others around the conference table may be asking themselves, "Who is she? How can we be through she'll follow through on this?"

Instead of watching your employees or colleagues while you're sitting on some type of cloud, get off it and out of your office and talk with others. No one is expecting you to make long-lasting friendships with anyone. In fact, that would be counter-productive, but you do need to know with whom you're working.

Keep in mind that you'll never be able to build a team that works together well and efficiently if you don't know the other members. Most importantly, the team will be most effective and your influence will be felt more if others see you as "just another team member."

A good word to keep in mind when you're building your personal professional relationships is approachability. It's difficult to have any influence if no one feels they can talk with you.

6. Actions speak louder than words

Always keep this in mind. Another good corollary to this step is the old saying that "talk is cheap."

Anyone can give a good speech or talk about their past glory days. That doesn't mean any of those words translate into action for today's issues or crises. The action of some sort is what others want to see. Some individuals are willing to see even wrong action in lieu of cheap words. At least they can see you're trying. Sometimes that's all it takes in certain situations.

You'll see work goes hand in hand with the idea of consistency. Once your colleagues and employees see that you're a consistent worker who gets results, your actions will then begin to speak for themselves. The concept behind this is to show others through your actions how effective your concepts are. Don't rely on your words alone to convince them.

7. Listen, listen, listen. Then listen some more.

Did I mention that a good way of applying influence in the workplace is to listen to others?

If you haven't guessed yet, listening is a vital instrument in gaining influence and developing into the leader others trust. One of the aspects of influence that hasn't been emphasized much is that it's a "two-way street."

Don't believe this? Then think about this. As you talk with your employees try to consciously discover ways to incorporate their viable and workable ideas into action. If they don't work, you haven't lost anything, but you have gained the respect and enthusiasm of those around you. If they do work, your employees will take notice and they'll be more willing to incorporate your ideas into their work habits. It'll be a win-win situation. And this is exactly what you're striving for.

Remember, though, that you need to take that first step by listening to everyone's opinions. Not only listen but be sure they know you acknowledge and respect their ideas. This is especially true of those individuals who normally don't go out of their way to voice their thoughts.

This whole process is useless if you approach it as just an academic assignment. You really need to listen intently to others, fully understand what they're saying and incorporate some of their ideas, if at all possible, into policy and actions.

If you keep these seven ways of applying influence in the workplace in your conscious, you'll be acting like the true and natural leader you are.

Conclusion

Gaining and maintaining influence in the workplace isn't as difficult as many make it out to be. All it really takes is an open mind and the willingness to listen and help your colleagues and employees.

Now, that you're familiar with the four principles involved in the process you may be thinking what took you so long to figure it all out. The important point, though, is that you have figured it out. And you have some indication of how to implement those principles.

While you may consider yourself well-educated in the process now – and you certainly are – there is still one more item to discuss. That is to be able to spot the difference between a "boss" who uses his title to get his employees to work and a true leader, who uses the power of influence and persuasion to reach and exceed goals.

There are two good reasons to be able to distinguish the differences. The first, of course, is when you're evaluating your own supervisor. Is he a natural leader, or does he depend on his title "supervisor" to get people to work for him?

The second reason you should be able to tell style from another is to keep your own actions in check. Yes, I know. You intend never to supervise; you'll lead all the team.

Even those of us with the greatest intentions at times fall into the "supervisor's mentality," and begin to think more like a "boss" and less like a true leader. You shake your head no now, but the longer you're in a leadership, the more the tendency is to fall into many of the habits of a person who depends on his title.

The following list of questions is intended to help keep you tied to how true leader think and acts compared with that a supervisor who because he has no influence relies solely on his title for his effectiveness.

You're thinking and acting from a boss' mentality if you:

1. . . . only see issues in black and white.

A true leader, on the other hand, recognizes the gray areas of workplace issues. He not only sees them but deals with them before they become big problems. The leader realizes that nothing is ever as cut and dry as it may seem on the surface and tries hard to plan for the shades of gray.

2. . . . prefer to stay in your office or chained to your desk.

The leader with real influence spends time "on the floor" discovering what his colleagues and employees think about issues. He's ready to talk to anyone at any time and is very often spotted with a group of workers around him.

3. . . . rule by fear.

That sounds harsh, but ultimately, that's really the only motivator someone with a boss mentality can use to get his people to work efficiently or take on extra goals. A leader, on the other, tells his employees the pros and cons of what needs to be done. Of course, the employees still may not like it but they'll trust the leaders view on the matter.

This is seen most often when there's been a change of corporate policy. No one may like it, not even the leaders. But the employees must act accordingly. Most people will put up less resistance if they know their opinion has been heard by at least one person – their leader.

4. . . . like to talk about what's happening or about what's to take place.

Sometimes, I used to think one of the qualifications for a good boss was the need to like to hear himself talk. I know better know. It may be those supervisors who are full of pride and overrate themselves like to hear themselves talk. But that's not what a true leader like.

Nor is it what a true leader does. He listens to his employees. This is true even if he's just given them an assignment with which they have issues. A true leader listens to his employees, then tries to address the issues as best he can.

5. . . . like to lay down the law.

The speech of a supervisor who likes to lay down the law would sound something like this: "Well, we're tackling this project from this angle because I believe it's the way it should be done. Period. And since I have to work in this office when most of you were still in diapers, I don't believe there are any good reasons to discuss this any further."

A true leader will listen to his employees' concerns. He'll follow up on what he can; he'll explain what can't be changed and why if knows. Guess who receives more cooperation?

6. . . . outline what is to be done.

A true leader will, of course, talk about what needs to be done. But he'll also take the time to explain why they're being asked to perform these duties. And then he'll listen to the employees concerns and try to address. If he can't, then he'll see if anyone else can and ask him.

As a leader, don't expect your employees to blindly follow you – especially if you all ultimately have the good of the project at stake. After all, they're the individuals implementing the project, they'll know best what will work and what won't. A good leader will listen and make changes if at all possible based on that conversation.

7. . . . manage to a specific outcome.

Now, that may seem like exactly what a supervisor should do. After all, how else would you get the work done? Managing to an outcome, however, doesn't take into account your company's greatest resource: its people.

A leader doesn't manage for a specific end even though it may appear that he does. No, his first and foremost thought is how to serve those people who trust him to do the right thing. He leads by serving others.

This may sound strange, Pollyannaish and even bizarre to some individuals, but I've seen it work time and again. It works in every setting from small churches to the largest of corporations. If you feel as if you're there to serve the needs of others, you'll be earning the trust, caring and the loyalty of your employees.

There are just seven of the ways a boss' mentality differs from that of a true leader. Keep this list handy as you gain your influence and practice you more fully develop your leadership skills. Anytime you feel as if you're falling into a boss' mentality, pull this list out and read it.

In the meantime, you can probably add more ways a supervisor's thinking differs from that of a leader. It may be you have a few pet peeves based on what you've seen where you've worked. If so, don't hesitate to write them down and look at them regularly. In this way, you at least have one way to gauge your performance.

Bonus: Thinking Outside The Box – Bruce Walker

Chapter 1: The Invisible Trap of Social Standards

Mary sat with her friends at the cafe. They were talking about their daily routines. "Sometimes I just get tired, believe it or not, of doing the same thing day after day. Don't get me wrong. I love my family and I wouldn't change them for the world. But, sometimes, I just think I need some spice in my life." She paused a moment and added. And I don't mean an affair."

Is that how you feel about your life? Do you look back at your high school days and even college days and think back to how much more creatively you thought back then? If you wanted to pack your suitcase and head for a trip to New York City or San Francisco or just wander aimless for a weekend, you'd do it.

Today, if you tried that there would probably a chorus of a thousand voices telling you socially responsible people just don't do that. You have to plan these things out. You have to make sure you get the right airline ticket price. And God forbid you take your car. What would happen if it broke down?

Even if you haven't yearned to travel you're probably like most of us, you approach it from just about every aspect of your life from "the box." Most of us are rather satisfied with this life.

Many individuals refer to this as their comfort zone. It's the area or activity in which they feel at ease.

This is the zone in which we accept who we are in life and where we are. After all, wasn't this the purpose of growing up and becoming an adult, to fit into society with a minimum of disturbance? And having a "comfort zone" is much better than constantly feeling anxious, feeling as if something bad is about to happen, but not knowing when or even why.

Comfort Zone or Stagnation?

But there's also a danger in that comfort zone and it's called *stagnation.* With that content, for some, comes the inability to see life any differently than what it is right now.

There's a theory that you're the average of the five people you associate with. What that usually means is you've adopted the social standards of these people. You've either adopted their interests or sought these friends and kept them because of your shared interests, similar careers or any other number of reasons. Support groups, by the way, are built on this concept.

If your friends are video gamers, for example, you're far more likely to be one as well. If they're interested in crafting, the chances are good that you'll be interested in that hobby too.

And that, is where the "box" comes in. As long as you're following the social standards of the group spend time with, you're probably not thinking outside of the box -- you may not even recognize that you're in a box. You certainly don't consider yourself "trapped." Or perhaps you do.

Either way, you're reading this book, which is probably an indication you're interested in jumping out of your box and getting out of your comfort zone. Why is it difficult for many of us to step out of our comfort zone, think outside of the box and think differently from the rest of the group?

When was the last time you stopped to think about what you really wanted -- and still want -- out of the life? Do you allow yourself to dream about an awesome vacation or starting writing that blog? Do others shoot your thoughts down right away, telling you it's a waste of time? So you return to your comfort zone and working within your box.

You do know it doesn't have to be that way, don't you? You can defy social standards and begin to do the things you've always wanted to do, the way you wanted to do them.

So, what's stopping you -- besides those so-called friends? Sure, their intentions are sincere, but ultimately you have to do what you feel is best for you. If you're weary of playing video games with them, tired of facing another scrapbook party without moaning and groaning about it or even can't take another episode of some "true crime" television show, then it's time to examine what's holding you back.

Here are several reasons why most of us are fearful of looking at life from any perspective than the one we've always have, that is our box.

1. But we've always done it this way.

Have you ever seen this sentiment in a poster:. "But, we've always done it this way." That is the biggest reason people resist change. In effect, they're saying that everything is perfectly fine the way it is. You'll hear this same sentiment expressed as "Why change horses in midstream?" This is their way of rationalizing their efforts to stay within their comfort zone.

You may have even heard the saying "If it ain't broke, why fix it?" These people are conveying the exact sentiment. The general opinion is that if something -- anything -- has served us well for so long, "don't rock the boat.". When you do try to change things or "fix" things, you may be making things even worse.

2. Trapped by your own personal method of thinking.

You along with everyone else around you may be locked into a familiar, comfortable way of thinking. Up until this moment, you may never have even thought about doing anything differently. Why, everyone around you is doing basically the same things and they seemed perfectly satisfied. Your dissatisfaction, you presume, only means there's something wrong with you -- not with the social norms.

Because of this, you approach your problems from a limited point of view. Of course, we have always done it this way -- who am I to even dream of doing it another way. You can blame your "inner critic" for censoring your potential "out of box thinking."

3. Trapped by your emotions.

Stepping into the realm of creativity -- especially if you haven't been thinking in that way for a while -- can be intimidating, to say the least. As you've already seen, you find yourself straying from your comfort zone. That leads you into an uncomfortable realm. It's here you're more than likely begin to feel a general anxiety growing. As you begin to think differently, you're entering an unknown world, filled with "what if" incidents. What if, one of those options you're considering is less than optimal?

Or worse yet, what if you take this momentous step and your friends and family think you weird? What, if after all is said and done, the outcome is embarrassing to you -- or even painful in some way?

What you may not realize that all of these emotions are just different ways your body resists change. It's hoping that you'll eventually cave in to these fears and qualms and just plain procrastinate on this concept -- whatever it may be.

4. It's hard to be creativity with personal problems hanging over your head.

If you're beating yourself up because you can't, for the life of you, think outside of the box, you may want to stop and examine your life for a moment. Are you going through some personal crisis or problem? It's hard to be creative when you're struggling with a major life change. You may be experiencing financial hardships at the moment or even going through an emotional event like a divorce. At these or similar points in your life, it's all most of us can do to just hold our own with the life we have.

Sometimes, though, this is the time when you may be digging up some of the oldest and deepest held regrets about what you *didn't* do with your life and you begin to daydream about "what might have been."

If this is the case, you still may want to wait to make any type of creative changes in your life. If you ignore these issues and continue to plow through with trying to be creative anyway, you may be just setting yourself up to failure.

5. Searching for the "right" answer

You've probably learned this habit in school. Every question, according the tests you've taken in school, has either a right or wrong answer. Think about the how many true and false tests you've taken and how many multiple choice quizzes you've sat through. After approaching an education in this fashion, you may discover your creativity stilted, at least initially, by considering whether what you're planning falls in one of these two categories either right or wrong.

Without a doubt, there are advantages to this categorization habit, but it does nothing to further your creative thinking. Right about now, you may be thinking that a three-week vacation to New York City is in order. But one of your dearest friends tell you this isn't the right time. That's not the proper decision right now.

Never mind the fact that this might be the "right" answer for you to clear your mind for a while. Or perhaps you've made a decision on some other aspect of your life, but here again someone or your instincts tell that isn't the "right" answer for you.

It hinders your "out of the box" thinking. Once you realize that the vast majority of issues we deal with on a daily basis can't be viewed in either black or white. There is a spectrum of shades of gray that can lead you to happiness. Issues that pop up in real life usually have more than one answer. When someone tries to assign a right or wrong way to a problem or try to impose one on you, they're missing the valued concept that the issue may have more than one "right" answer.

6. Viewing creative, outside of the box thinking as "destructive."

Here me out on this one. Perhaps you don't even realize you're thinking this, it may be so ingrained and enmeshed in your thinking. If you choose a different way of doing even something as simple as changing your morning routine, your subconscious may feel that it's being a destructive force in the world. After all, if someone wanted to point at you and accuse you of ripping the fabric of society as we know it apart, he might be right. "Rules," they may say "are that simple and are created for a reason. Who are you to deviate from them? What makes you special?"

You may believe, at first glance, that this is a block that makes little or no sense. But you'd be amazed at how many individuals follow all the rules, even though they aren't working for them. There's a person I spoke to once who said before she takes any specific actions she asks herself, "How does this serve me?" If it doesn't serve her -- make her life better in some way -- she tosses that "rule" aside. Step by step, she's remaking her life in a very creative way, by thinking out of your own box.

Have you noticed that that people praise and admire some of the most creative thinkers in the business world? Think about Richard Branson and his marvelous success and the brave moves he made to make it happen. But they refuse to break even a small rule in their life. Perhaps you should think twice before you start admiring someone like Branson -- and start breaking some rules of your own.

Seriously. Are you ready to consider not only thinking outside of the box, but actually kicking it wide open and allowing some truly creative thoughts into your life? Then you're ready to move to the next chapter. That's where we'll get the process moving.

Chapter 2: Kicking the Box Open and Sparking your Creativity

Many people get excited about the idea of thinking outside of the box and kick it to the curb immediately only to discover that after years of conventional thinking, it's a bit more difficult than they had imagined. And that makes sense. After years of thinking one way, it's not easy to allow your mind to be "liberated" and allow it to run wild.

Before you attempt to jump into creative thinking, you may want to "exercise your brain." Don't worry, these aren't as tough as you may believe. It's hard to start thinking in a manner you're not accustomed to.

To be truthful, that's not your fault. So don't beat yourself up if the creative thoughts don't flow immediately. Your brain has been used to thinking in a certain manner and it will take some time for it to rewire itself and adjust to another thought process. It'll be slow going at first, but as you continue to do it, your brain catches on and works faster at it. Guaranteed.

Your brain is no different from any other muscle in your body. If you don't use, then it slowly gets weaker. That's the bad news. The good news, though, is that it's easy enough to strengthen this muscle just as you would any other one in your body: through regular exercise.

At first, when your "creative thinking muscles" are initially called into action after perhaps years of unused, you may turn around and find yourself wandering aimlessly through your house, wondering where and how to begin this valuable thought process.

Many fiction writers find that every morning upon arising they need to get their "creative juices" flowing by writing three to five pages of . . . well, nothing. Their goal is to write anything that pops into their minds. Hopefully, some of this covers what their subconscious minds have unearthed while they slept. But if they can't recall what they dreamed of or any words that came mind then basically, they're instructed to write anything. It may be something as simple as "I need my morning coffee."

Once they clear their minds and got their neurons moving in full speed, they inched themselves out of their box and into their projects, whatever those may be. Believe it or not, it works more often than not.

Best Way to Active Your Creative Thoughts

If you're not by nature a writer, you obviously you won't need to do this (although it still may be a wonderful creative exercise for you as well). But if you're not interested in writing, here are few alternatives that may help channel your creativity more efficiently.

Alphabetize your Words

Okay, they don't have to be *your* words but once you discover this exercise, you may very well become addicted to it. It forces you to look at words in a different light, which can only help you begin to look at not only words differently, but the entire world around you from a new perspective.

Begin by picking a word, any word will do. It may be one you've just noticed on a billboard while you're driving or something you discover on a magazine cover. Now instead of looking at it with your physical eyes, look at it with your mind. What you're about to do is rearrange the letters so that they're placed in your mind in alphabetical order and not as the word is spelled.

If the word is "number," then you'd rearrange the letters like this: b-e-m-n-r-u. This makes your mind use all the information, but just rearrange them. Don't just settle for doing it once a day, though. Remind yourself to do it throughout the day. Consider doing this up to five times a day.

When you first start off, you may want to choose short words. This activity is a bit harder than you may think. As you conquer words that are three to five letters long, then you'll graduate to ever longer words. There's no need to push yourself, you'll discover that if you just allow this to happen, you'll have more fun. And part of thinking creatively certainly involves fun.

Another note for you to think about. No one need to know what you're doing if you don't want to tell them.

Adding a series of one-digit numbers as quickly as you can

This is another exercise that on the surface doesn't seem to have any connection to creative thinking or thinking outside of the box, but after you do this for a while, you'll discover how your synapses move more quickly. That's a sure sign, you'll be thinking creatively without even having to think about it.

Take a series of one-digit numbers, from zero to nine. Place these numbers in any order you care to. Now, without using a calculator, start adding up the numbers -- as quickly as you can. The beauty of this exercise is that it forces you to constantly change the information you're juggling in your mind. As you're adding this total, your mind needs to focus solely on the current grand total -- and then as you become faster at this -- another grand total quickly. Talk about making your brain agile.

Basically what you're doing is inputting some essential information into your mind and then deleting it -- replacing it with another "grand total" as you add more numbers -- and so it continues. The perfect time to do this? When you're standing in the grocery line. You can easily add up the numbers to one of the dollar of five dollar bills you have in your pocket or just as easily take the numbers from your purchases and use those numbers -- in no particular order.

Before you realize it you're performing this action faster and faster. But the true goal of this exercise is to limber up your creative thinking.

Running for creativity.

Now this suggestion may be the most confusing of all. It is for many individuals. On the surface, it really is difficult to see how the creative process is connected to exercising. But running is wonderful because it stimulates your whole body, producing the chemical called *serotonin*. It's been called the "chemical form" of happiness. Its long been known by scientists and medical doctors to be responsible for that "runner's high" so many individuals talk about.

Once you hit that "runner's high" your mind is capable of seeing things from a different perspective. You're much more likely to see the whole picture of the issue. Researchers now agree that the combination of what many call "the runner's point of view" and the increased blood flow pumping throughout your body actually improves your concentration. This is especially helpful, because your mind is churning out solutions and ideas that only you can perceive.

Carry a notebook

This may be simple, but power habits you can develop to encourage yourself to think outside the box. Carry a notebook. All the time. No exceptions. Have you ever come up with an idea and say to yourself, "Awesome. I'm sure I'll remember this." By the time you get home or to someplace to write this idea down, it's slipped your mind, with no guarantee to return.

It may be that none of the ideas one day are extremely useful. But that "not-so-useful" idea may lead you to another wonderfully useful thought that may be the one to change your life.

Eat dark chocolate and walnuts

You have to wonder how this suggestion can possibly affect your ability to think outside of the box. But, even if it doesn't, it's a tremendous method of rewarding yourself. If you don't like walnuts, don't worry about it. You can eat Brazil nuts or almonds and get the same creative effect.

Why would dark chocolate and nuts increase your creativity? You can thank the rich and abundant supply of antioxidants found in this combination of sweets. These wonderful substances enable your blood to flow to the brain more swiftly which in turn improves your concentration.

Additionally, the nuts are a great source of vitamin E which prevents poor memory and increases your concentration levels. By the way, eating this combination of food also increases your happiness.

Adopt the Beginner's Mind

You may believe you're ready to tackle the world with your out of the box thinking. But there's still one more exercise you'll want to think about while you're using these activities. It's called adopting the beginner's mind. At least that's what the Buddhists call it.

Some people refer to as a looking at life through the eyes of a child. You can call it whatever you desire. The idea is to empty your mind of everything you believe you know about your world and how everything around you operates and look at your surroundings as if you've never seen any of it before.

Remember when you were a child, anything and everything was possible? Think back, too, to when your children were younger, they too saw the world with eyes of wonder. Absolutely nothing is impossible. And that's exactly how you should be looking at your world in order to think outside of the box.

Don't feel constrained by what worked in the past or what gave you grief. Try it again. It just may work this time. And even if it doesn't, it may be the idea that leads you to the one that will actually change your life.

This is more difficult than you may believe and it may be one of those exercises you need to repeat not only daily but several times a week. Eventually, you'll come to every issue with a "beginner's mind," realizing you really don't know anything about the issue. Finding a creative answer is so much easier this way.

Here is an exercise in what it feels like to look at things around you with a beginner's mind. Gather the following items: a coffee mug, pen and paper. Yes, that's all you'll need. To have a real good time doing this you may want to invite a few friends to join you.

Place the cup on the table. Give yourself -- and your friends -- a specific amount of time. It's best to set a timer, then no one has to stop to watch the clock as the minutes tick by. You know that a coffee cup's purpose is to drink out of.

But what else could it be used for? You've seen people use them as pen and pencil holders among other things. List as many of these uses as possible. The goal is not to limit your thinking. If your first thought is a house for a mouse write it down. The sky's the limit.

Walk Away from the Problem

Seems counter-intuitive now doesn't it? But it works, nearly every time. Walking away -- either literally or figuratively -- and clearing your mind for a few minutes seems to clear the mind enough to allow your subconscious mind crank some idea out.

Try it and you'll see. This trick works probably for the same reason that you get your best ideas in the shower. You're allowing your mind to clear and busy with an activity that is done by rote memory.

Anything that makes your mind relax and "digest" the problem, as it were, helps you to think creatively.

You're almost ready to apply creative thinking in your daily life. There's only a few more steps you should know about before you can expect great success from your "out-of-the-box" thought processes.

In the next chapter, you'll discover how a thought process called "lateral thinking" can work hand in hand with creative thinking to help you take that grand leap out of the box.

www.ingramcontent.com/pod-product-compliance
Lightning Source LLC
Chambersburg PA
CBHW070352190526
45169CB00003B/1007